Game on M

C000151999

Paul Casnmore
Copyright © 2022 Paul Cashmore

All rights reserved.

ISBN: 9798352459799

The advice heron is not intended to replace the services of trained health professionals or to be a substitute for medical advice. You are advised to consult with your health care professional with regard to matters relating to your health, and in particular regarding matters that may require diagnosis or medical attention. Neither the author nor the publisher can be held responsible for any loss, claim or damage arising out of the use, misuse, of the suggestions made, the failure to take medical advice or for any material on third-party websites.

DEDICATION

To my three beautiful children who inspire me every day. You make me smile and I love you with every fibre of my being. The greatest gift in life and my greatest achievement is being a Dad. To my incredible family whom I love and adore who have been with me through the highs and the lows. To my wonderful friends and my best mate who is literally a walking spiritual Guru. To those that have come into my life for a reason, a season or a lifetime I am grateful for every moment we share and have shared. To those that are reading this book, welcome to my square peg in a round hole mind. This book is dedicated to you all.

CONTENTS

SYNOPSIS

Written by Paul Cashmore the badass fugitive Hunter from the Channel 4 series Hunted on how he fucked up his life, overcame chronic anxiety, got his shit together and became a spiritual guru.

Well I didn't actually become a spiritual guru, or am I a Badass but by being in the darkest place you can get I had to deal with some shit, well a lot of shit to be fair but the biggest thing I had to sort out was my own worst enemy. MY MIND.

Your mind can be your best friend or your worst enemy and it doesn't matter if you have the most loving and caring partner, or the most supportive family, if you have been taken over by your mind and your internal dialogue is fucked you can only get better when YOU decide to. In my case, it was too late to save some aspects but what I did manage to save was my own mind.

From begging to have my head removed and someone press reset, to having tests on my heart, to not being able to breathe through chronic anxiety to literally pressing the nuclear button on my loving family. In this book, I speak openly about how I dragged my ass up, and absorbed everything and every bit of help to get myself back to being a good man. I speak about the link between spirituality and science, how I got my nutrition on side, stopped drinking alcohol and some weird synchronicity through what is known as the Law of Attraction. Now, this stuff really freaked me out.

We all make mistakes in life but every morning we have the chance to start again. Change your diet, lose weight, start a business, and become the best version of yourself, whatever it is you can do it.

Now whether you want to read this book to feel inspired or have a read about how someone who on the outside appeared to have it all yet was internally fucked I am sure you will find something of value.

A little warning though I do swear. Apparently, it's a sign of intelligence. So if you are not easily offended by the occasional F Bomb and fancy a rollercoaster read I am very grateful. If you take anything away from this book I want you to know it's never too late to start again and become the best version of yourself and be the change you want to see.

PREFACE

The breakdown is often the tipping point that precedes the breakthrough, the moment a star implodes before it becomes a supernova.

How true is this?

Life is throwing stuff at us constantly to test us where at times we are thinking "Just give me a fucking break" and we focus on the negative emotions that are consuming us. We are living in survival mode in a constant state of stress from the moment we wake up to the moment we fall asleep. Our minds race and replay the fuck ups and mistakes we have made, the shit job, our finances, our weight, the news on TV, and social media flooding us with fake news (so said a former President) which causes shit chemicals to surge through our body.

So, Monday morning arrives, and we are filled with dread. We make it to Friday, get pissed, feel like shit Saturday morning, do some chores, get pissed on Saturday night, feel like shit on Sunday and become anxious about Monday morning.

Sound familiar?

A bit extreme I know. But I have written this book to tell you that anyone can struggle with life at any time. I don't care what background, how successful, or how much money you have or don't have, stress, anxiety, and depression can hit anyone and I mean anyone. Including me. On the outside, it looks like I am living my best life. Featured as a Fugitive Hunter on TV and a happy family man, yet internally I am malfunctioning on an epic level. When asked if I am OK, my response is "I'm Ok" which is most people's response, especially a guy. Men have this fucking dumb ass mentality that if they are struggling with life they can't speak out because it will make them sound weak. But let's be clear, physically I'm not weak, but internally it's my mind that is misfiring. In this book I talk about how stress and my internal dialogue almost cost me my life, it cost me my family and how I overcame it. The techniques I have learnt, how I became more aware of spiritualism and science and how they are now becoming more aligned and how I got my shit together.

If you are struggling right now with any aspect of your life and this book resonates with you and inspires you, I want you to know that by the end of it I hope you get up on Monday mornings like a fucking Lion and seize the day and every day for the rest of your life.

If however, you're a nosey fucka and just want to have a look at some dumb shit I've done and whether I articulate myself then good times, I hope you enjoy the journey and thank you for reading and welcome to Cashmore's journey into my crazy unicorn world of tofu crocs and tree-hugging.

I don't hug trees (not publicly) I actually don't, but what I have done is embrace change. Yes, I am still a potty mouth, yes I still take the piss, yes I still train hard, but yet I have also embraced a more spiritual side. Compassion and kindness is not weakness and telling someone you love them is extremely powerful. Saying sorry and admitting your mistakes is a road to feeling free and being grateful for even the small things in life will turn your entire world around.

If you know me and see my writing style go off on tangents then you know exactly where I am coming from.

I hope this book resonates and you can create a life that is fulfilling, has meaning and is filled with purpose. You can set your goals with clear intention and be so fucking driven every day that when you wake up you are filled with fire and excitement that your goals and aspirations are going to be annihilated. That you understand that there is no such thing as an overnight success but everything comes to you at the right time.

I believe no one in this world should be suffering especially in their own mind. Your mind can be your best friend or your worst enemy. Once you understand that then holy shit now we are going into something next level.

As the phrase goes 'Be the super hero of your own movie'.

I want everyone one of you to envision your future self with excitement, ditch the past but learn from it, and focus on kicking today's ass and moving forward towards your goals and dreams. If you need to get your finances together, take it head on, if you want to lose weight, it starts TODAY. Don't put off until Monday or tomorrow what you can start today. Be consistent in your approach.

I am not perfect. Not by any way shape or form. You will read about how I have fucked up but I have learnt the lessons. About how adopting certain beliefs and strategies helped me get my shit together.

We could also play a game. You know the one where you would go to a village fete and guess how many sweets are in the jar. You could try and guess how many swear words I use in this book. I honestly don't have a clue. I guess I could count them and the winner gets a pick n mix. I don't use the C word (pretty sure I don't) but I do drop a few F bombs in the mix. It's the way I articulate myself. I could try and justify myself using these words as I am sure I read that it is, in actual fact a sign of intelligence. Thank you Google, I will roll with that. Some of you reading this will be saying "But Cashmore you can't write! Did you use dot to dot or colouring crayons"? I hear ya loud and clear. Even I surprised myself that I smashed out a few thousand words.

But part of my journey is to **Do What I Said I Would**. No procrastinating, no more self-sabotage, just get shit done and be a fucking good man and if I've learnt anything, it is this. If you are lucky enough to find a weirdo never let them go.

Forever grateful
Paul

THE BREAKDOWN

If you are reading this book I want to thank you and if this book resonates with just one person then I hope it provides the inspiration to turn your life around and that you will find happiness and success.

Why did I decide to write this book? People look at me and think I'm this tough Hunter from the BAFTA-nominated television series Hunted and super successful when in actual fact I want to be honest with you and tell you that if you are struggling with life then you are not alone my friend.

We all make dumb decisions, trust me I've made some epic-level dumb decisions so don't beat yourself up. The reason we make dumb decisions can be a number of factors. Ego can be one of them. You make dumb decisions to impress people that have no bearing on your life whatsoever, you make dumb decisions because you are living in survival mode and under constant stress and you are living in what is known as 'fight or flight mode' and then there is living in past trauma and practically self-sabotaging everything because you believe that you don't deserve to be happy.

FUCK THAT........... YOU DESERVE TO BE HAPPY!

Let me tell you from first-hand experience I have probably ticked all of those boxes. Shit decisions and most probably self-sabotage and living in stress where my mind has literally misfired on an epic level. When I was given the advice to seek help, journal, meditate, and exercise you can literally do all of these but I soon learnt a harsh lesson that none of them works until you find self-love. Now anyone out there reading this and has just read 'self-love' it is either going to resonate with you or you are going to say "Cashmore are you for real you absolute hippy?" Unless you love yourself, and I don't mean in an egotistical narcissistic kind of way, I mean to be kind to yourself, talk to yourself with positive affirmations instead of negative self-talk as we all know now through quantum physics and the placebo effect and what science is showing us, the mind is an incredibly powerful tool and does not know if you are joking or not, you must not speak negatively to yourself. It is proven that the mind can heal you, placebo experiments have shown this. The mind my friend can be your worst enemy or your best friend.

How do I know your mind can be your best friend or your worst enemy? Well, it's not just from reading books but it is from first-hand experience of making shit decisions. Now don't get me wrong, procrastinating on a decision or making no decision is worse than making any decision, but if your health is fucked, you need to make a very big decision to fix you. If you are not firing on all cylinders you are pretty much no good to others.

Let's get real here. I will be open and honest and tell you that not long ago (at the time of writing this)I pulled out a pin on a grenade in my life. I hit my ultimate breaking point. There is no point in writing this book with the hope of helping and inspiring others unless I admit and tell you about my own journey. There are countless people out there who on the surface appear fine and internally are in so much pain. Men are a nightmare for this. There is this stigma to be a tough character and that it is weak to cry or feel sad or stressed or talk about how you feel. Then what happens? That pressure cooker lid starts to go but there is nowhere for the pressure to escape. Some drink alcohol or take drugs, some find some short-lived pleasure to get a quick dopamine hit and some do the unthinkable and commit suicide but thankfully the vast majority get help and come back stronger than ever.

The build-up to mine wasn't just one thing it was a multitude of scenarios that had built up and I was spinning plates and finding it extremely difficult to keep spinning them and now my internal dialogue was fucked and my health was declining. Lets now throw into the mix a tight chest, racing heart rate going from 55 to 179 then dropping down rapidly, inability to breath and then to a point where the strength had gone from my hands and my body wasn't working to which my colleague thought I was having a stroke. So when you then hear that some friends and colleagues have died of a heart attack and one friend who went to sleep one night and didn't wake up I was pretty much now of the mindset if I don't sort this shit out I'm going to go to sleep and not wake up. The catalyst was on my driveway begging for someone to remove my head and press reset, the pain was so unbelievably unbearable.

If any person has a breaking point I had hit it with the force of a raging tsunami. I had said for far too long " I'm OK" which was bullshit and I was now in a position where my Monkey Mind was in control. This is where it becomes terrifying. When the Monkey Mind has hold of the chariot of your life, you are now in a battle to get back control before you crash and your chariot explodes. The Monkey Mind feeds you with a barrage of shit literally coming at you like missile fire and you are trying to dodge them and also fight to get back control. You are now in a war with your own mind. I was being hit with some serious negative self-dialogue, holy shit, then images would flash in front of me like a picture book of scenarios from childhood, from my life as a police officer, if there was shit to be dug up and thrown at me, my Monkey Mind was like "BOOM have it motherfucker". I literally broke my own heart into a thousand pieces and drove to York to my brothers. I'd say pretty much by the look on his face he was worried. So the pain in my head and the pain in my chest and the inability to breathe were now in full swing. How the actual fuck am I going to pull myself out of this? I thought life would be much simpler if I had broken bones or lost a limb because then it's something physical and you can see it and justify it. Now not only did I have a shit tonne of plates I was spinning and stressed, but I am now proper fucked. If there is a higher being, a God or whatever religion or belief you have I prayed for a miracle. My Dad called me and was non-judgemental and said "You can do this, you're a fighter" but honestly I had no more fight in me. When I say the tank was empty it was empty. Crippling anxiety is a massive drain on your energy resources and when it kicks in full swing and you try to fight it there's nowhere to go, you literally fuel the anxiety fire. What you think is how have I gone from being a confident, driven, fit and healthy man to this? It is completely bewildering. I found that I was extremely lucky in that my friends and family didn't judge me. They listened to me go on pretty much like a broken record and most days I wasn't looking for an answer as everything in my head was a big old jumbled mess. What I really struggled to understand and comprehend is why I sabotaged my loving relationship. Now I am über confused, I feel emotionally drained, physically fucked, extremely sad, guilty, embarrassed, ashamed, and worthless, it was like walking around in concrete shoes.

I had watched the Tyson Fury documentary about how he went from being depressed and overweight and crying on his knees praying for a miracle. That came into my head and then a quote about imagine there was a documentary crew following you around and that you can have your own comeback story. Be the guy who is sat there in tears looking to end his life, making protein shakes from leftover pizza, I had the image from films where the main character is fucked and loses everything and he makes a comeback, I decided at that moment I had to make the biggest comeback of my life. I had to become the man I once was, I had to inspire others, be that loving, supportive partner again, an inspirational Father figure to my children and a monster when it comes to my work, determined, focused and on a mission to fucking rebuild the shit storm I have created. My life is completely in the fucking toilet right now, but it is time to get up, show up and take the first steps.

So what do I do? Now I am not saying that I am a champion boxer but the first thing for me was to train and train hard. It was time to put on the shitty battered old tracksuit, grow a beard and work out in a barn. Well not quite like that but I had to drag my ass up, forge a battle plan and move forward. Move forward with determination and make the biggest comeback of my life. I had to prove to myself, to my incredible friends that support me, my wonderful family and those that have been affected by all of this that it does get better and that whatever life throws at you you can come back stronger than ever. A monumental task for sure and certainly not as easy as I thought. You can't just turn a switch and automatically be Mr Jazz hands again. You can't automatically be forgiven for upsetting those that love you but what you can do is fucking be humble, accept your flaws, admit your mistakes, apologise (and mean it) and DO WHAT YOU SAID YOU WOULD!

BLAME

We can all sit here and blame everything else in our lives, the circumstances, our childhood, shit decisions, shit relationships, shit job blah blah blah so the first thing I had to do was take ownership. I had to own everything. We all have free will. Sometimes we make the right decision sometimes a shit decision. It's owning them. I also had to ditch the anger I was holding onto about previous decisions and circumstances. Not as easy as it sounds but forgiving others is extremely powerful and liberating. Honestly, I used to be angry, with a nickname called 'BASH' hardly surprising where that came from. I'd be forever in punch ups. I had no fear of losing and my mate in the boxing gym would say "You're nuts, you take 2 to land one". It was like I needed to be hit to get me fired up. Naturally, in my normal state, I would say I have a reputation for being extremely patient and calm. Being hit, and punched, none of that bothers me and I think I relate that back to my childhood. I was a very quiet, shy child brought up by my mum. I was naturally strong but terrified of social situations. I stuttered when I spoke fast and I was like two different people. A quiet, shy, calm boy to someone who is extremely confident. I loved wrestling with the older kids down the street from me. There was this family a few doors away that had older twin boys and me and my mate would wrestle in the garden with them and I would love it. It literally brought me out of my shell. I'd give as much as I got. I'd have them in headlocks and try and choke them out, it was completely nuts. We only had one pair of boxing gloves so we would fight each other just wearing one glove, literally beating the crap out of each other on the driveway.

I digress……. I'm trying not to be all Ronnie Corbett and tell a story and go off on tangents. Anyone who doesn't know what I'm talking about, Ronnie Corbett was a comedian and part of the 2 Ronnies from a TV show in the 1980's. He would sit on a chair and tell these funny stories to the audience and would deviate from the story. I'm sure there are clips on Youtube.

Now where was I?

So blaming others. I would allow others to have so much bearing on my life and emotions its unbelievable. Once I identified and refused to give that power to another, it was game on.

It literally is Game On Mutherfuckers.

A couple of people and scenarios I allowed to affect my state and they thrived on it. It fuelled them to know they had triggered me and what is funny is when you don't rise to it, shut it down and don't give it the time of day, you are literally sending that energy straight back to them and they have failed on an epic level. You find yourself at peace.

Whether it is Buddhism, Stoicism or any other religion or belief the one thing that stands out to me is that it's not the situation or circumstance but our reaction to it. Powerful stuff huh? We can all find blame in something. A co-worker, partner, job, whatever it may be, we find ourselves in this negative downward spiral. Once you are in control of your reaction to the situation, you my friend are entering next-level peace. Don't get me wrong there are still fuckwits in my life where I can hear the ludicrous shit coming from their mouths, but now I don't even entertain it and find it quite funny the absolute drivel that is coming from them. That shit gets shut down. People can't hold a facade for too long until the demonic freak reappears and gives you a reminder that "Yep they are still a whole bag of fruit and nut".

Most of us act as if external circumstances make us happy. A delusional materialist thinks being a millionaire will bring lasting happiness. But what about someone who seeks happiness in family, nature or improving the world? Buddhism explains that happiness comes from within, not what you are experiencing, but from how deeply or mindfully you are absorbed in that experience.

I have only just really started to embrace meditation and am staggered by the scientific data and the health benefits. The first benefit is stress reduction. Normally, mental and physical stress cause increased levels of the stress hormone cortisol. This produces many of the harmful effects of stress, such as the release of inflammatory chemicals called cytokines. These effects can disrupt sleep, promote depression and anxiety, increase blood pressure, and contribute to fatigue and cloudy thinking. Research has shown that meditation may also improve symptoms of stress-related conditions, including irritable bowel syndrome, post-traumatic stress disorder, and fibromyalgia. I mean this is incredible.

Meditation is shown to thicken the pre-frontal cortex. This brain centre manages higher-order brain functions, like increased awareness, concentration, and decision-making. Changes in the brain show, that with meditation, higher-order functions become stronger, while lower-order brain activities decrease.

In 2005, Harvard neuroscientist Sara Lazar began to publish some mind-blowing findings: Meditation can literally change the structure of your brain, thickening key areas of the cortex that help you control your attention and emotions. By 2014, there had been enough follow-up studies to warrant a meta-analysis, which showed that meditators' brains tend to be enlarged in a bunch of regions, including the insula (involved in emotional self-awareness), parts of the cingulate cortex and orbitofrontal cortex (involved in self-regulation), and parts of the prefrontal cortex (involved in attention).

One study found that 8 weeks of mindfulness meditation helped reduce anxiety symptoms in people with generalized anxiety disorder, along with increasing positive self-statements and improving stress reactivity and coping. Meditation may also help control job-related anxiety. One study found that employees who used a mindfulness meditation app for 8 weeks experienced improved feelings of well-being and decreased distress and job strain, compared with those in a control group.

What does a mindfulness meditation practice often involve? You sit down, close your eyes, and focus on feeling your breath go in and out. When you feel your attention drifting to the thoughts that inevitably arise, you notice, and then gently bring your attention back to your breath.

Now this isn't an excuse to say to your spouse or partner "Hey I'm feeling a bit stressed so I'm just off to do a meditation" then sheepishly skulk off for a little snooze. Well, you could, and quite frankly I don't blame you. Who doesn't love a cheeky little Nana nap in the afternoon? Dive under the duvet, shut the door, phone on silent and say a big "fuck you cruel world".

When I first started doing meditation it was like a formula one race in my head. Holy shit what on earth is going on here? Remember the original Batman series? They'd be kicking and slapping each other and you would see "POW POW" pop up on screen in cartoon writing. This was my mind. "POW" "KAPOW" "POW" 'BLAM" Jesus Mary Joseph and the Wee Donkey I am never in a million years going to be able to pull this off. Then if I tried to meditate and lay down, I would be that exhausted I would actually just fall asleep.

Which to be fair, because I wasn't sleeping on a night so this was a welcome break.

ANYWAY. I have persevered and attended the Buddhist temple close to where I live and it's like a light bulb moment. What they teach you about happiness and your thoughts is completely true. During a 90-minute class, we do two 10-minute meditations and the Monk talks to us. It's so calming in their presence and when you complete a guided meditation you leave feeling like the world has been lifted from your shoulders. Now if you are someone that is deeply unhappy, gets pissed, eats shit and thinks that going to the pub and acting like a full-on clown is making your life a dream and you are unwilling to embrace something that will benefit your life then fair enough. A lot of people (mostly guys) will not make changes or do something that they feel will make them less of a man. I would hear stuff like "I'm not doing that hippy shit", which is OK. If that's your identity then it's OK. But if deep down you want to make your life better and you are a character of something you are afraid your friends will 'take the piss' out of' then you need to grow a pair and do what is right for you. Or you will be absolutely fucking miserable for the remainder of your life.

IMPRESSING OTHERS

We spend our lives trying to impress others. Whether it's through social media, the clothes we wear, the car we drive, or the house we buy, we strive to get validation from others. The really fucked up thing is we want validation and likes from people we don't even know on social media apps. THIS IS CRAZY! Why on any planet would we care about some fucking moron called johnBfishpants96345 who comments on your post? This is probably some absolute fruitcake sat at home eating a sandwich whilst masturbating over a wildlife magazine. I mean come on. We take selfies and post them so we get likes and comments of "Oh hun you look amazing" or we post something like "Having a shit day today " or a cryptic one like "Fuck my life" and we get responses like "Oh Hun DM me" "Oh Hun sending love and hugs". Fuck off Barbara I haven't seen you for 35 years since we were at school. If I messaged you asking to drop me off some food because I'm unwell you'd shit yourself.

Social media can be massively detrimental to your mental health. Multiple studies have found a strong link between heavy social media and an increased risk for depression, anxiety, loneliness, self-harm, and even suicidal thoughts.

When you receive likes, the brain interprets that information as a "reward" and releases a rush of dopamine. This "pleasurable event" leads to doing it again: you share more content and wait, glued to the screen, for new reactions. So a lot of selfies are seeking a Dopamine hit that will make you feel better. So the next time you post a selfie or see a selfie try and look at why. Why am I posting this selfie? Why did that person post a selfie? Chances are that person isn't feeling their best and needs a dopamine hit and this is coming, the majority of the time from people they don't know or give a shit about. Because if your life was in the toilet would these people help? Probably not. Look, I've done it. My ego has said "post a selfie and let's get a dopamine rush. Ooh, look someone said you look great. Then how many times have you looked through your feed and thought holy shit I don't look too clever in that photo or actually my eyes look sad? Or how about this one? How many people do you know put up selfies with their partner saying "My rock, my world" knowing fine well they had a massive fallout moments before? I know people who have posted couple photos where they declare their love for each other and the person who posted it is having an affair. I know first-hand people like this. So next time you look at social media and feel all down in the dumps because of the 'hot couple' or people living their best life, just take a moment and think 'are they really?

I do dip in and out of social media. I personally find it quite stressful. We all want our photos and lives to look great. We want to portray an image. I feel like I am bashing social media here when I don't mean to, but what about when you post social media stories? I find this hilarious. So I can put up a photo and most probably get the same average number of likes but if I put up a story, the view count goes off the hook. The same old names look at my story but never interact with my images. Welcome to the social media stalkers. I love doing this. Boom, there she is. Boom there he is. It's almost instantaneous. They just have alerts. I imagine them working and getting an alert to a story I've posted and them fumbling around

22

spilling their coffee desperate to see what I'm doing and it's a shit picture of nothing relevant like a chocolate wrapper. Fookin hilarious, there she is right on cue. I should tag these people in a story and watch them freak out. I seeeeeee you.

Anyway, what I'm saying is, who gives a shit what people think? Stop trying to impress others. That's your ego screaming at you to do it. If you live your life seeking validation from others it is going to be a really long and lonely existence. There is a difference where we selflessly help others and are there for them but do not live our lives seeking the validation of others. Once I came to this realisation and did not care about the opinions of others I had a massive shift in my mindset. It is like a huge dark cloud lifting from you. I started asking myself why I was giving away so much power to someone else and allowing them to affect my emotions. Whether that was triggering anxiety, sadness, anger, or whatever it may be. Once you realise this and take that control back you will be flying. I mean literally flying. There are people out there who seek to trigger you and you know exactly who they are. Provoke you, smear campaign you. Ex-partners can be a classic example or ex-in-laws. How many people out there have had an ex-partner try to stop you from seeing your children? This is one of the cruellest ways to trigger someone in my opinion. So many examples of this. All they are doing is seeking to hurt you. This is an extreme example but one I am very aware of. Let's use the ex-partner as an example. If you are getting provoking messages saying you are this that and the other and you respond with venom, then the venom continues. If you ignore it, then you are not fuelling it. The Buddhist Monk said if we respond with "OK" and let it go, we can just let it go. The idea of just letting go, taking a step back and breathing is liberating. If you have tried to make peace and the other side is unwilling to make peace then so be it. Be grounded in peace knowing you did your best.

This isn't about impressing others but it kinda leads me to find peace in conflict. Now I've been in my fair share of conflict. Some conflict was work-related whilst I am trying to protect others and some conflict is in my own life. This is normally where I have made some shit decisions, been selfish or the other party is a fucking absolute cockwomble. So on my journey of mastering my mind, I have looked at the shit decisions I have made. So some scenarios where I thought I had made a shit decision were the best fucking results I could have made. Sometimes what we think at the time was a shit decision or a painful experience turned out to be a blessing. Whether it's the universe or guardian Angels stepping in, who knows? I'll give you an example. I am about to start a business with someone who I thought was a good friend. But something kept niggling at me that something was wrong. I have always believed we all have a sixth sense and that there is something else in this world other than this 3D life. There was an ache in my chest and a whisper in my ear but I used to think it was me just being paranoid. So anyway my gut was telling me not to trust this man and then boom, he butt dialled me, whilst talking about me saying the business doesn't need Paul. Holy shit balls, thank you universe. I felt crushed but also kinda smug that I was right and wasn't being paranoid. The shit part was I had to work with this person on another project and again turned out to be a fucking lunatic and throw me under the bus to save his ass. What this person didn't know is never to underestimate someone who is a bit quiet. This person is taking note, banking everything and protecting their ass from an incoming shit storm. As they say, The loudest one in the room is the weakest one in the room.

I have now though started paying much more attention to my intuition. That shit is will save your ass more than you know.

INNER GUIDES

This is where we lead nicely from the previous chapter into a more spiritual side. Before you flick past this section please hear me out. I used to ridicule this and take no notice, yet would get nudges all the time and signs and signals, yet I chose to ignore them. The millennials out there refer to the power of thought as 'The Law of Attraction. Now, this shit is trippy. I have read numerous books including Dr Joe Dispenza and watched documentaries such as HEAL and this stuff is fascinating. Your mind is a supercomputer. We can't dispel it anymore. The simple way of accepting this is the placebo effect. How someone can heal or have pain relief from a sugar pill is mind-blowing. How many people have changed their mindset and healed from chronic illness? Equally, with our negative thoughts, we have made ourselves poorly and attracted shit scenarios.

One of the most trippy examples of manifesting or even being helped by your spirit guides is when I was a Police Officer. I was part of a Robbery team and would drive around in an unmarked Police car, in my case those who know me, was a silver Vauxhall Vectra. This car was great. I had the best time driving this battered old thing. We would get an incoming call, blue light gets plugged in and put on the roof, headlamp flash and hidden blue lights in the grill. It was like something from Starsky and Hutch. I'm running around with my mates wearing jeans and an Abercrombie T-shirt like we owned the place.

So we are in the office and someone said to me "What would you do if someone was pointing a gun at you?" I replied with Johnny Big Balls "I'd run them over". If this was ever a sign to prepare for something then this was it. On this certain day, my team and I had to drop one of the members at Kings Cross train station and then I and 2 other team members would carry on from there. So we dropped him off and then it came over the radio that Officers from the TSG (Territorial Support Group) were chasing suspects towards Grays Inn Road. Holy shit that's around the corner. So on goes the blue light, and I slowly go against the oncoming traffic on Grays Inn Road awaiting commentary from the Officers chasing the suspect. I decide to hold on a junction to see if they will come our way. The blue light from the roof is taken down and seconds later, holy shit there is the suspect and he opens fire. This guy is probably only about 20 metres away. People are ducking and scattering out of the way as he tries to hijack a London taxi. The taxi driver puts his foot on the accelerator and the suspect runs in front of our car. Now all of this is happening in lightning-quick time but you see it in slow motion. My mind is slowing down. How the actual fuck am I going to stop this? I have no gun. I have no bulletproof vest. All I had was a radio and this trusty Vectra. The suspect still carrying his gun runs past our car and pulls a member of the public from their motorbike. I spin my car around and we are now face to face. Me behind the wheel of a car, the suspect crouching down about to escape on a motorbike and pointing a gun straight at me. I hit that accelerator and the gunman went under the car and I landed the wheel on his chest. Thankfully stopping where I did otherwise I would have been in a whole world of shit and likely killed him. My team get out of the car, uniformed officers emerge and I reverse the car off him. Unfucking believably he is still fighting. What on gods earth? The next thing to do is contain the crime scene. So I grabbed cordon tape and then the realisation kicks it. I look down and there is the handgun. The magazine had fallen out. Holy shit that's a real gun. Thankfully by the grace of God or whatever you believe in, when he was pointing it at us he had run out of bullets. As I walk around further there we go, there are bullet holes in a door. Now the chances of this happening are very very slim. I'd even say you have more odds of winning the national lottery jackpot. The chances of being asked and then it happens, well who knows. My friends and colleagues would say I had a guardian Angel and maybe that's true. But only now since I hit the ultimate rock bottom in life do I wholeheartedly believe it. There are a tonne of examples and my mate John would jokingly say when I was in his offices that if I was in bad mood then his computers or electronics would not work. I would laugh it off but when you start reading books about Quantum Physics and energy not woo woo books as some like to call them, you understand that everything is energy.

Energy is everywhere. It's invisible. Things that are solid like your chair are energy. Everything is made up of energy. When you break atoms down into subatomic particles, there you have it. It's just energy. Energy is everywhere. So much so that our own energy can be measured 3 ft from our body, but the scientists say that is the limitation of the equipment.

"Everything is energy and that's all there is to it. Match the frequency of the reality you want and you cannot help but get that reality. It can be no other way"

Albert Einstein

This is not new. It is also known as Chi in China and as Prana in Sanskrit. Science has now caught up and shows us that everything is energy. It is the building block of all matter. The same energy that comprises your body is also the one that makes up the bricks of the house you live in. If we are thinking positive thoughts it can influence those around us, causing a ripple effect in the energetic ether. It's like a boomerang. What you send out comes back to you with a stronger force. If you are sending out positive vibrations, reflecting your true emotions and feelings, then the 'boomerang' will come back to you with positive events, people and circumstances, which we often view as 'coincidence'.

The same goes with negative emotions and thoughts such as worry, anger, hate etc. The 'boomerang' will catch up with you sooner or later and return your negativity through experiences or events.

Religion and science are fast approaching each other. From a scientific viewpoint, we see experimental evidence suggesting that we are all part of one energy and universal consciousness.

Nikola Tesla, one of the greatest ever minds said "If you want to find the secrets of the universe think in terms of energy, frequency and vibration".

Our brains pulsate with electromagnetic energy that is affected by our emotions, our health and our general state of well-being. If an energetic force is struck at the same resonant frequency as another object in a facility the vibrations will cause the second object to begin vibrating. In terms of how you experience the world, the energy and vibration you give off are met and reflected back.

We can feel this on an emotional level when we say that somebody is on our wavelength, or we feel in tune with a person or situation. Why is this important? If your internal vibration is one of anxiety, depression, or anger, the life experience you have, may very well provide you with people and situations that reflect this back at you. Thereby reinforcing the feeling and so creating a negative experience for you. It's a bit like tuning into different radio waves. Depending on what frequency you emit, will decide on what station you pick up. What is clear from modern research is, sound, can at the very least affect matter.

In the 18th century, Ernest Chladni put sand onto a glass plate and vibrated it with a violin. The sand was poured into creative and beautiful symmetric patterns. This work has been continued with the invention of the cymascope by John Reid, who uses water as a surface membrane in which to imprint sound and create a digital representation of sound and vibration.

I would play classical music for my children when they were babies and studies show that Mozart helps brain development. It is funny how music has such a profound influence on your emotional state. It can trigger so many emotions. Music for me is like a photo. It triggers memories, feelings, and emotions, that can inspire you, make you feel sad, feel energised to destroy the gym or put you into a calm meditative state. I have come across binaural beats that play at a certain frequency for the brain. This stuff is amazing. I was trying meditation and playing one of these. I wasn't asleep but so relaxed in this meditation that I heard this female voice say "Oh no you've Overdosed. Wake up". I desperately tried to open my eyes but couldn't move any part of my body. What probably took about ten seconds seemed like an eternity. I was so far into it that my body was really in a relaxed state. Not going to lie, I did have a mild freak-out. So if you didn't think I was bananas you probably do now. But wait until you read the rest of this book. It gets even more trippy.

LISTEN TO YOUR BODY

So one of the factors in my epic meltdown was my heart was pretty fucked. I started getting chest pains and the only way to describe it is like someone putting their hand underneath my rib cage and squeezing my heart. I went to see the Doctor and was initially prescribed BETA Blockers (which I didn't take) I would go to the gym and be on the cross trainer and see my heart rate increase to 179 BPM and then drop almost instantaneously by 60 BPM. Now I initially thought that this was because the handles on the machine were sweaty and weren't reading my heart rate correctly. Then I would notice it change on my watch. It would spike and then drop. What on earth is going on?

I was referred to Glenfield Hospital to have tests and also sleep with a heart rate monitor strapped to my chest. I had blood tests and all the results showed I was OK and didn't have a heart condition.

Now what? I watched a documentary called HEAL. Now, this is incredible. What a documentary and if you watch anything and haven't seen it, please do. It has some incredible contributors with examples being Bruce Lipton and Joe Dispenza and Greg Braden.

They cover the placebo effect, and energy healing and a phrase I had to explore more was 'HEART AND BRAIN COHERANCE'. What is this? How it works is that your thought is the electrical charge of the quantum field and feelings are the magnetic charge, so how you think and how you feel broadcast a field. Once you change frustration, anger, resentment, to joy, freedom, gratitude etc your heart starts to beat coherently like a drum and produces a magnetic field. That energy is a frequency, and that information is your thought which can be carried and broadcast.

I wanted to go a bit deeper and a bit more scientific which brings me to physics and realise that we are all energetically connected and this is called 'ENTANGLEMENT'. So in quantum physics, particles remain connected so that actions performed on one affect the other, even when separated by great distances. Albert Einstein called it" spooky action at a distance."

Now Physics alone is beyond my pay grade never mind quantum physics but I find it fascinating. I have tried to understand it. When photons are miles apart and yet they are connected this isn't just airy-fairy stuff this is science. You can think of the twin phenomenon, how two separate beings can think and do the same things. That is right there in front of you. So if entanglement is real, quantum physics is real, brain and heart coherence is real and measurable maybe we all need to start listening to what our body is telling us.

We are not designed to be happy we are designed to survive. Not a hundred percent sure why I just dropped that sentence in there but I'm leading onto something, trust me. If our first and foremost 'instinct' is to survive then we should be listening to what our body is trying to tell us. I think our heart is first, then our gut and then our brain. Let's make one thing clear. I am not a Doctor, I am not a spiritual guru I am a man that ended up having a massive breakdown and trying to pull myself out and tell you how I did it. What works for me may not necessarily work for others.

So our gut is also known as our second brain. Some would argue it is our first brain Your gut and brain are connected physically through millions of nerves, most importantly the vagus nerve. A study by Professor Nick Spencer at Flinders University maintains that ENS (Enteric Nervous System) in the gut is the 'first brain' and that it evolved long before the brain as we know it. I also read that a troubled intestine can send signals to the brain, just as a troubled brain can send signals to the gut. Therefore a person's stomach or intestinal distress can be the cause or the product of anxiety, stress or depression. That's because the gastrointestinal system is intimately connected. So when we experience "butterflies in the stomach", this is the brain in the stomach talking to the brain in your head.

So your thoughts affect your emotions. But what about if your gut is out of balance, can this affect your mental health? Before I delve into this question, my physical health was normally pretty great but one thing I have had that is so painful is kidney stones. Holy shit when I say painful, I mean I'd like to think I have a pretty good pain threshold but man alive these things are next level. Doctors normally compare it to the pain of childbirth. Now the female contingent are next level hard. If you can give birth and bounce back like it's a walk in the park, then I give you my ultimate respect. Men can't even get a cold without it being 'MAN FLU' we are so different. But anyway I digress. Kidney stones. These can be brought on by several factors, being dehydration, foods rich in oxalate and animal protein. So that's when I decided to go on a journey of trial and error and eliminating foods and trying to find out if I can change this and not go through that pain again. I spent Christmas in hospital with a 7mm kidney stone stuck, urinating blood and feeling like shit, but ended up in a ward next to some extremely poorly people with life-threatening illnesses which in retrospect made me feel very grateful.

In your gut, serotonin plays a role in processes including digestion. However, the changes serotonin makes in your gut may also send signals to your brain that affect the production of neurotransmitters there. In the brain, serotonin is involved in mood and sleep. Your gut bacteria also produce the neurotransmitter GABA, which helps reduce stress, anxiety and fear.

I would regularly be having a swollen belly, some days my face would look like a tomato, or I would have unexplainable pains in my feet and body and tightness and my joints would feel stiff. Then I would be fine. I would just be so confused thinking how is this possible? But could there be something that I need to fix in my gut? Mental health conditions like anxiety can be linked with chronic gut conditions like IBS and with scientists identifying specific gut microbes that may be connected with mental health conditions. One study found that people with depression had fewer of two types of bacteria called Dialister and Coprococcus in their guts. Study participants with more of these bacteria reported higher scores when researchers asked them about their quality of life.

So if what we feed our mind is so important to our mental health then what we feed our body and our stomach is also important. The first thing that had to go for me was alcohol. The link between feeling shit and drinking alcohol was huge. Unless I was absolutely hammered and fell asleep into a coma, my sleep would be shit, I would feel like shit, I would look like shit. Alcohol is a depressant. It may reduce your inhibitions and when you go out you have a great time, quite possibly end up sleeping with someone you instantly regret and then have a whole world of pain come into your life. Or you would drink and then start crying. Or you would drink and get angry and turn into Johnny Carpet Arms wanting to fight everyone. Or become depressed. The funny thing about alcohol is the peer pressure when you don't drink. The response from so many people is "OK what's wrong with you?", or "Aren't they boring!" Well, my thinking now is, if you need to drink to not be boring or let your hair down, then who exactly is boring? Now I am not bashing those of you who enjoy a tipple or two. We all make our own choices in life, I just decided to not drink because I feel like shit. I get headaches and want to pull my head off. What I find utterly bizarre though is if I go out to the pub or wherever and I now choose not to drink that I have pressure to drink. Anyone reading this who is trying to transition to a healthier life and not drink, just do it. Ignore those that pressure you into doing something. I guarantee they will leave mulling over why you look better, why you are flying in the gym, your clothes fit better and they feel like shit. I've heard all the excuses, you have a shit day at work so crack open a bottle of wine, or you are cooking in the kitchen and crack open a bottle of wine, it becomes an association in our subconscious programming which becomes our default go-to.

So I have dipped in and out of not drinking. I am not saying I will never drink again but when I don't drink I feel so much better for it. My eyes look bluer, my skin is better, I sleep better and I couldn't give two fucks if you think I'm boring. No problem my pedigree chum. I can think better, I can think clearer and to be honest, if I am ever in the pub for a social event and Johnny Carpet Arms with his pint of wife beater wants to for whatever reason fold me like an origami swan, I will probably be in a better position in sticking one on his chin rather than picking from a mirage of three heads because I'm hammered. Also if you are a Peaky Blinders fan Tommy Shelby stopped drinking, so if it's good enough for Tommy it's good enough for me. Also when you don't drink you are so much more attuned to things that are going on. I was massively intuitive before, but now I have taken it to the next level. I know I have said it before but my intuition is normally 99% bang on. Sometimes I just can't pinpoint it and would think it is because I am a paranoid android or is my intuition alarm going off. If it's my alarm I just bank it now until I corroborate it with something else. All right, Sherlock calm down. I've lost count of how many times I've been right all along. Pretty devastating really, but we are wired for survival. If you are on autopilot driven by your subconscious you will miss it.

Anyway back to ditching alcohol. So now that's gone I have also been on the fence about my nutrition. Man must eat steak, sandwiches, drink pints, eat shit........ Do they? Well let's be honest, I used to think the same. If I was training I would eat animal protein, I loved cheese, bread, and drinking Port, but hold on a minute. Let's just have a look at this. When I did my PT course and nutrition and learned about macronutrients, protein, etc what makes us fat and feel like shit is too many calories and not moving enough, and the devil of all things is sugar. Not fruit or carbs, but refined sugar found hidden in so many products. Not rocket science. But after having kidney stones and watching the many documentaries I decided I would do my own experiment and try a plant-based diet. I have interviewed many people and what stands out more than anything is the compassion aspect of eating an animal, the impact on the planet and the number of antibiotics and shit that is pumped into the animal. I would be consuming this and putting this into my body. So if my gut is out of sync, my brain is out of sync and stress is hitting me from everywhere I think it's safe to say I need to get shit sorted. Stress massively affects your gut so much that there is something called 'Leaky Gut Syndrome' where toxins can end up leaking into your bloodstream and have a major impact on so many health conditions.

NUTRITION

Why is nutrition so important? Well, it's not just what we feed our minds but what we feed our bodies. When I touched on imagine there is a documentary film crew following you around and your life is in the toilet and you're blending last night's pizza with some protein powder and chugging it down with some eggs, well it's not exactly like that but I was in and out of what I would feed my body. Should it be animal protein, should it be eggs, should it be fruit, should it be that massive bag of Monster Munch from the petrol station, or that ice cream or eating until I am in a carbohydrate coma? Here we go, this is it, I've hit the nail on the head. Emotional eating. Anyone who wants to lose weight will come up and say "I don't have time", "But I love Macaroni and cheese" or "it's Friday which means Pizza night". So you end up during the week on a calorie deficit eating shit that doesn't light up the reward chemicals in your brain and then BOOM it's Pizza night and your brain is on a massive high. You savour every bite until your stomach is expanding and you look 9 months pregnant and then start beating yourself up. Not in the physical sense where you are looking in the mirror saying "you looking at me" and then punching yourself in the face, nope, it's that self-loathing I wish I hadn't eaten all of that pizza because my clothes don't fit. So why do we do it? Let's look at my own personal journey.

If I had a goal and a vision and something to aim for I would be disciplined like most people who are getting ready for a wedding or an event, but if it is mostly just day to day and you are cruising along, the majority of people have no real incentive when you can easily just buy bigger clothes right? Are you happy? Well actually here's the thing. If you are happy in your own skin you have hit the jackpot right there.

It's not about weight or aspiring to look like some cover model because let me tell you they don't look like that all year round and are in such a calorie deficit that they become miserable. Weighing their food, watching every macronutrient, and becoming so obsessed to the detriment of their family home is not good. Find a balance. We all know it's calories in versus calories out, but It is also the quality of those calories. Sugar, which is highly addictive can send you on an emotional rollercoaster and you feel shit or stressed. How many of us want to smash a bar of chocolate to feel better? I do. Oh hell yeah. Even though I was relatively good with my nutrition it wasn't on point as it should be. I am not telling you what to eat, I am just using myself as an example. I have ditched animal protein for several reasons. Environmental impact, health reasons and compassion and I feel much better. I have become the king of blending smoothies and am no longer of the mindset that fruit and carbs make you fat. What a complete clown for believing this. Carbs are the body's preferred source of energy and whilst we need fat and protein I can still get these from plant sources. Excess carbs that turn into glycogen and nowhere for it to be stored will inevitably be stored as fat but you have to be nailing some serious calories and sugar and sat on your arse for this to happen. If I do an hour of training on the assault bike I probably could burn around 700 TO 1000 calories and become depleted. So HELLO family-size bar of chocolate. Only joking but so what if I did have some?

Back to the topic at hand. Why is nutrition so important? Well if you've read the previous chapters and not skim-read the book because I am incredibly boring you will know about the gut-brain link and how important the gut is in our overall health and our mental health. So because I was so gone and in the darkest place I have ever been I made a promise to myself that I would never ever go back to that place again, and if this was going to help then so be it. While learning and understanding plant-based nutrition I decided to document my journey and interview health professionals including Doctors and athletes and also had the blessing to interview a chef called Derek Sarno. Derek and his Brother Chad started Wicked Kitchen and Derek's inspiration for doing this is so emotional and inspiring. He was a chef cooking everything including animal protein and making great money until his life was turned upside down. His fiancé was tragically killed in a car accident and Derek's life went into a downward spiral. He ended up in a Buddhist temple to help him recover and he began cooking for the monks and learning about compassion for all sentient beings and creating vegetarian meals. Now this man is a genius. He cooks these incredible lion's mane mushrooms and has a cookbook and Wicked foods are now in supermarkets. The brand isn't what you think. You can still be a badass and throw in a few F-bombs and still be compassionate. So they have inspired me, even more, to be creative and cook and enjoy the experience of adding flavour and creating delicious food.

The next reason I decided to give up is I interviewed Alice Brough a former pig vet and one of the team who took the government to court to try and put an end to factory farming. The conditions these animals are kept in are horrendous and the amount of antibiotics and shit pumped into these animals so we can eat them is mind-blowing, so now my mind is made up. How can I sit here and feed myself knowing horrific suffering has happened, also I am fuelling my body with this. At what point is this a good idea? Some of you you will be reading this thinking I have hoodwinked you into trying to convince you to become vegan. Not at all. I am not here to try and convince anyone to do anything. The whole premise of this book is to document my journey back and what I have done and what works for me doesn't necessarily work for others. Only when someone is ready to make changes for themselves will they do it. But what about this for a sobering thought? Processed meat is a class 1 carcinogen. This is as bad as smoking! How the actual fuck can food which has been classed the same as smoking be sold in shops? We can feed this to our children. You know when you are diagnosed with a chronic illness and it is through a lifestyle choice you realise that you have the free will to make a difference. Our bodies rejuvenate and repair every 7 years. We have the chance to make a change in our lives at any point. Some of you might be reading this out of pure curiosity and want to know how did Cashmore fuck his life and what's that loon up to, some of you have no idea who I am and want to know that there are people out there who have turned their life around and feel inspired to turn your life around. At any given point in your life, you can make a change. A change in career, your mindset, your health but you have to want to do it for yourself. If you are met with resistance, that's OK. Seriously if want to eat a Buddha bowl and avocado then do it. Equally, if you want some chocolate, do it. Just find a balance and do what is right for you. I love chickpeas. Who doesn't right? Well, I found someone. My brother Steven. I made us both dinner and found out he is the only human walking the earth who doesn't like chickpeas. This is a phenomenon and one where I need to refer him for brain scans and testing. If anyone else doesn't like chickpeas let me know. We can set up a club for you, ha.

My morning consists of coffee first. Yep, that's right. All the fitness and health gurus out there who say you should drink water first thing and do yoga and have an ice bath, whilst deep down I agree with you, coffee is the number one thing in life. THE NUMBER ONE THING IN LIFE. Period. But it sets your heart rate higher, messes with your adrenals can increase anxiety, and whilst all of these have sound scientific backing if I remove everything in my life that provides me with a modicum of pleasure I really am going to be sad. I love the smell, the taste, how it gives me the sense of life isn't so shit, after all, well maybe not the last one, but you know what I mean. But it stops you from absorbing iron...... Look if you're a health guru and your brain is now going bananas on the negative impact of coffee let me come back at ya. Coffee apparently can reduce the risk of developing type 2 diabetes, could support brain health, promote weight management and decrease body fat.

Reduce body fat you say. Errrrrr yep yep yep. The numero uno ass-kicking property of coffee is fat busting the midsection. I will roll with that all day long as justification for my morning cup. Plus my coffee machine is the coolest gadget I own.

LIFE WILL GET BETTER

I keep reading the heartbreaking news about people committing suicide from people in the public eye to old school friends to people I had encountered during my time as a Police Officer. One lady I saved from suicide had cut her wrists and was about to jump off the balcony of the 17th floor of a tower block. I managed to talk to her and she let me join her on the balcony and patch up her wrists and eventually she came back inside. I accompanied her to the hospital where she received wonderful care and support from the NHS staff and made an excellent recovery. The second lady I saved from suicide tried to jump off a bridge in North London. I decided to grab her as quickly as possible and get her to safety. Again I went with her to the hospital where she received excellent care and help. My point here is no matter how difficult, how overwhelming the situation you are in, there are people and charities and support out there, so you should never feel that you are alone!

Data shows that males aged 45-49 continue to have the highest suicide rate. Now whatever gender you are, no one should ever get to a position in life where the only option in life is to commit suicide. We see it in the news about celebrities taking their own life with the tragic news of Gary Speed and Caroline Flack. The news and social media are flooded with #BEKIND and comments of "I wish they would have just spoken about it."

I do believe that no one wants to die, they just want the pain to stop. How does someone go from being driven and motivated to having anxiety and chest pains? This is where I will be honest with you. I was exhausted from having Anxiety. Whether you believe in divine intervention or God, something kept getting me up. Boom I'd have an anxiety attack, wherefrom I had no idea, and I would carry on. Boom, another anxiety attack. Then I would carry on. Boom chest pains. Carry on. I was literally like "Give me a fucking break"

If you want an example of divine intervention here's one for you. There is a Pastor in America at the Red Rock Church called Sean Johnson and I came across this video completely by accident. I wasn't looking for it, and in it, he says he was about to commit suicide because he couldn't take the pain of anxiety anymore. He is praying for protection for his wife and their 'boys'.

Now when I am praying for a miracle and this shows up by accident how am I supposed to believe that this was a coincidence. This guy isn't what you would expect a Pastor to look like either. A handsome looking guy, dresses well, I mean seriously. What are you trying to tell me? Is it God, is it divine intervention, is there a calling, is it the universe, is it my guardian Angels? All I can say is that I am still standing and still fighting and I am thankful every single day for everything and everyone in my life.

Is there a lesson in everything? Have I been taught a lesson? At the time of writing this, I am only four and a half months after the breaking point. I have accepted my mistakes, I have apologised with every heartfelt emotion to those I have hurt and whilst I can't change history I can use this experience to be a good man. A good man going forward and if there are tests and God wants to keep throwing these tests at me until I have learnt the lesson then I understand.

Certain things and situations would keep coming up and I believe they will keep coming up until you learn the lesson.

If you are struggling with life at the moment, trust me, it gets better. Don't be fooled like I was into thinking it will happen overnight. It doesn't. It takes time. I messaged the church to thank them for sharing the content to inspire others and had a zoom call with them and found out Shawn had written a book about anxiety. Safe to say I have now downloaded the audiobook and will listen to it on my travels.

What I want you to know is, that it is now you're time to shine.

It's time to get up off the canvas and be the superhero in your movie.

This topic isn't the most cheerful part of the book but I want you to know how precious life is and that we all have a part.

If we backtrack a bit to where my working life started at 21 years old I became a Metropolitan Police Officer. I moved from York to London and what an eye-opener that was. I thought I'd seen it all and got the T-shirt, when in fact I'd seen nothing at all and got NO t-shirt. London is nuts. Everything is open 24/7, it's busy 24/7, tube trains are crammed, buses are crammed. I mean if you want to be a Copper then join the Met. I hadn't been in that long when I saw my first set of body parts on a train line. Walking along I saw a foot, then a thigh, then a hand. I mean this isn't a film set this is real life. When you're new, one of the jobs that gets assigned to you is that of a sudden death where it's a non-suspicious circumstance and you have to wait for the doctor and undertakers. What stays with you is the smell. The smell of death is quite haunting. You definitely can't be squeamish. No training school will prepare you for death. I've been present at post mortems and that's enough to mess with your sleep.

The reason I'm touching on the rather morbid topic of death is to remind us that life is precious. We get one chance so why not give it a good go?

One night when I was about to go off duty a call came over the radio that there had been a stabbing on an estate in North London. Unfortunately, there were no units available to respond so my mate and I jumped into a car in our plain clothes with nothing but a radio and made our way. Upon our arrival it was chaos. The young man who had been stabbed was lying on the floor and an angry mob had now formed. Between the two of us, we managed to commence first aid, cordon the scene, and establish witnesses where a nickname of a guy was mentioned as the suspect. As more units arrived I coordinated a sweep of the area and the knife was recovered. I went with the victim to the hospital and despite the best efforts of the hospital staff, unfortunately, this young man's life was cut short. I recognised the nickname of the suspect having arrested him many years before and after a subsequent investigation he was convicted. I remember while I waited with the victim the family desperately tried to get to him to hug and kiss him. In an instant, this young man's life was taken from him causing widespread devastation to his family.

I want you to remember that life is short and it can be taken away from us in an instant. So embrace each day, find things to be grateful for and begin your action plan for world domination.

So why do I say find things to be grateful for? Well if you are going for world domination or find your side hustle or Find your Dharma, which is your life purpose, you need to shift focus from complaining to a more positive attitude.

When we think of all the stuff we hate, those valuable minutes, hours or days dwelling on the negative things in life, we could put that time to much better use. Most people say they don't have time, they're tired, yet can quite easily get home at 6 pm, eat dinner, and watch tv all night moaning that they have to get up early for work. Now couldn't that time be spent more productively?

First find things that lift your spirits. make a vision board, make a folder on your computer with images of how you see your life, places you want to visit, a watch on your wrist, the car you want, the house you want to live in whatever it is, you need to visualise those things and tell yourself daily you are now on a mission to get it. Be grateful for life. It doesn't matter if your bank balance is low, your current home isn't the one you want, your partner is abusive, just remember life is going to change and will change as long as you want it to.

Time is something that waits for no one. If you have zero funds or you are the wealthiest banker it does not matter because one day time is going to run out. That is the one fact of life that we cannot change. Time will eventually run out. We are born and then we die, it is what we do in the middle that counts.

Now this book is for anyone and I mean anyone. Where you are right now does not matter one bit. I'm going to tell you right now it does not fucking matter one little bit. Many people have become successful later in life so don't use age as a bullshit excuse. Even if you want to re-educate yourself or retrain it's possible even if you are broke. You just have to put the time in and be patient. This is what most of us lack though. PATIENCE. We want everything now. We want 6 pack abs in 2 days, we want to lose 7 lbs in 7 seconds, to win the lottery, patience is key my pedigree chum. It took me over 20 years of knockbacks, festivals to make it into television and be in Hunted. Whatever it is you're going to pursue, be patient. It will come.

So what qualifies me to write a book about becoming the best version of yourself? I know what it is like to have crippling anxiety attacks, I know what it is like to have everything and I know what it is like to have nothing. One of the most common things people mention when they hear that someone has taken their own life or suffered from anxiety is "Oh my God I didn't know, they always seemed like the life and soul of the party and always smiling". On days when we need to turn it on we can be Mr and Mrs Jazz hands and make others feel better and when the spotlight has gone, curl up into a ball and sit in total darkness and quiet. For those out there struggling right now, there are so many people and organisations that can help you. Mind Charity, Anxiety charities, your Doctor, friends, and family, just speak out. The first step to achieving an incredible life is to ask for help. It's the first small step to an incredible future.

LIST-MAKING

Your brain can literally become a pressure cooker and unless the lid is released and the pressure is taken away you can spiral into a very dark place. Just talking about things helps enormously. There could be trauma from years ago, historic life events that can cause Post Traumatic Stress Disorder, financial worries, family breakups and trying desperately to see your children from a previous relationship. You will be surprised by what help there is out there. But being in a state of constant stress is going to cause you major problems.

What is stress?
Stress is your body's way of responding to any kind of demand or threat. When you sense danger—whether it's real or imagined—the body's defences kick into high gear in a rapid, automatic process known as the "fight-or-flight" reaction or the "stress response."

Your nervous system responds by releasing a flood of stress hormones, including adrenaline and cortisol, which rouse the body for emergency action. Your heart pounds faster, muscles tighten, blood pressure rises, breath quickens, and your senses become sharper. These physical changes increase your strength and stamina, speed up your reaction time, and enhance your focus—preparing you to either fight or flee from the danger at hand.

Chronic stress disrupts nearly every system in your body. It can suppress your immune system, upset your digestive and reproductive systems, increase the risk of heart attack and stroke, and speed up the ageing process. It can even rewire the brain, leaving you more vulnerable to anxiety, depression, and other mental health problems. Now I am not a Doctor and if you are struggling, my advice now is to seek professional help and consult your GP.

When I decided to write this book it was with a view, that through my experiences I can inspire others to believe that no matter what you are going through, what you have been through or what you you are about to go through it will work out just fine.

So how have I managed to turn it around? Well, the first step is to change your mindset. When you focus on the negatives your body is in a negative vibrational state and produces chemicals like cortisol. If you are constantly stressed and your body is producing too much cortisol and derails your body's most important functions and can lead to several health problems like anxiety and depression, heart disease, trouble sleeping and weight gain.

If we are feeling constantly stressed and we find ourselves purely focusing on the negative situation or circumstances the problem is never going to go away. We all know what we need to do to find a solution but most people just run on the hamster wheel and can't get off.

Here is another lesson I learned. Trying to purely focus on positive thoughts alone won't work. This is your conscious mind working. The conscious mind works at 5% of the day, with your subconscious mind processing and controlling 95% of the day.

What would happen if your subconscious programmes matched the wishes and desires and aspirations you hold in your subconscious mind? Twice a day your brain is prepared to download information and this is where you can reprogram your subconscious mind! Learn this and you will have the life you want! The subconscious mind is a habit mind! There are two ways to get programmes into that subconscious mind.

The subconscious mind is operating at a vibrational frequency of THETA which is hypnosis. So when you are in this state you can download this information. So apparently twice a day your brain goes through a period of THETA. When is that? So when you are sleeping your vibrational frequency is in DELTA and as you start to fully wake up and you're not fully awake now this is a period called THETA. But as you awake you then become into an ALPHA state, you're doing your routine and when you start your day you hit BETA which is active consciousness.

When you come home and you slip into calm and get to Alpha and you start to get ready for bed your brain starts to go from ALPHA to THETA as you start to fall off and go to sleep. Could this not be the time to listen to something or read something?

Also when we are older we learn differently by habit and rituals. Repetition is key. When you repeat something there is a point where it is in the subconscious mind. Like the lyrics of a song. You hear it long enough it is there, riding a bike, learning a language, simple repetition and it is there, downloaded. So what is it you want to download? If you want to make a change it starts with repetition until it becomes a habit and then bingo. They do say it takes 30 days to change a habit and most people have no patience right? We want it done now. But as the saying goes patience is a virtue. That's why I have adopted meditation to quiet my mind.

Some technical stuff about brainwaves huh? Who would have

thought I would have been writing about that? But let's talk more about repetition and use losing weight as an example. I've helped so many people with trying to lose weight and the best thing ever is not the training it is the mindset. Always 100% the mindset. Without question. You can take these principles and apply them anywhere. At this moment in time, you are conditioned. You are conditioned by your subconscious mind. You wake up, get ready, do your work, eat your food, come home, tired and sit down and watch TV. I'm not generalising everyone here, but hear me out. In between all of this you look at social media because it's so fucking addictive. A cheeky snack sat on the couch watching some murder documentary that scares the shit out of you and has you checking to see if you have locked the back door. We are conditioned. To achieve our goal, we have to change our conditioning and mindset. All the thoughts of I will do it Monday, Diet starts Monday, I'll do it when I can fit into my gym clothes, I'll do it in January, I don't have time, I have 6 weeks until Barbaras wedding so will start in a couple of weeks and do the Beetroot juice diet, come on have a word with yourself. I'm not saying I am not a procrastinator, I was king of procrastination and would put off shit tasks because they didn't excite me or they terrified me and filled me with anxiety. But here is the thing I have learnt my lesson. Those things that you put off, once you start or tick off, you get a massive rush of feel-good chemicals and feel amazing.

When planning something a strategy that is often used is writing down SMART goals. SPECIFIC, MEASURABLE, ACHIEVABLE, RELEVANT AND TIMELY. You can use this if you want to get all specific and have short, medium and long-term goals. So if the goal is to lose 4kg in weight (body fat) then a strategy can be put in place for your eventual goal which includes milestones. With this, you see progress and see it is working. No quick fix, no overnight success, but with consistency and repetition, you will smash your goals. No one who is not a runner is going to one day say "I am going to run 10k". They are going to start walking and slowly building up the run.

Tweaks to nutrition will be implemented. Then before you know it, a 10k run has been smashed.

Consistency is key. If you focus on being overweight or unfit or your clothes are tight, remember anything can change. I use exercise as an example because this is probably the number one therapy I used. I did a mixture of cardio and resistance and one of the bits of kit I love is the assault bike. This is normally used by Cross Fit trainers and I built up to use this thing for an hour. Sweat dripping from me and because it was cold steam would be rising from my top. I would be playing music but I would have moments where my mind would wander and all of a sudden some of those negative thoughts would start to creep back in. Hold on a minute Tiger, you can fuck right off, I have endorphins flying around at the moment, this is hammer time and knock those thoughts out of the park and replace them. I learnt that, rather than challenge these thoughts and get into an argument with myself, and not a verbal one whilst on the assault bike, that would be weird, I would simply replace the thought. I use this technique a lot now. So when you go through a traumatic event or scenario I find that it can replay in your mind like a vivid photo book with visual images popping up. I would simply acknowledge it, let it pass and then replace it with something else. It is the same with missing someone. I stop focusing on missing them but hold a fun memory or running on the beach, falling over and laughing.

We have a tendency to purely focus on the negative and the things that have happened to us. Our brains are wired for survival and seek out any threat, danger for shit scenario so it doesn't happen again. We aren't wired for happiness we are wired to survive. Back in our ancestral days, being wired for survival would be running from a sabre tooth tiger, but now it's so many things.

KICK START THE FEEL GOOD

The best starting point is making a list! List making is the best thing to do. Write down everything that you want to sort out, that you want to change, that you want to achieve. You can even separate them into categories. Making lists of small tasks like mowing the lawn, hanging a photo frame to cleaning the car will make you feel a real sense of achievement once you've crossed them off the list.

The second thing to do is find things to be grateful for. Now you might be in complete shit street at this point and thinking there is fuck all I'm grateful for but trust me that's because you are focused purely on the shit. Once you start being grateful you'll have an energy shift. So it could be something as simple as having a cappuccino, a roof over your head, clothes to wear, your children, whatever it may be, find something to be grateful for. The friends you haven't been in contact with, the family members you haven't called for some time, give them a shout and ask how they are. It is amazing how doing something for others or simply checking on their well-being will inadvertently make you feel better. Now if you're thinking "Well what about me" trust me that's not going to flip you out of the negative vibration and get you off the hamster wheel. That's because you're in a poor me mindset. If you take interest in others they will take interest in you.

So what is it you want to change? Just start by going through every aspect of your life and brain dump it onto good old-fashioned paper. When 40 little things are swimming around in your mind they become a big problem and we struggle to know where to start. If you are in a shit job and waking in the middle of the night worrying then trust me my friend you can change it. There is no reason whatsoever that you cannot get another job, retrain, learn a new skill, or start that business you've always dreamed of but please don't let fear cripple you. Don't let fear be your enemy. Let fear drive you, embrace the challenge and be so fucking driven and so utterly confident every day you wake up as a lion. The word 'failure' does not even exist. That word simply means your action plan didn't quite go according to the plan you envisaged but you're so adaptable and so focused and so driven that you can overcome any hurdle and change tact.

I have lost count of the fuck ups where shit didn't quite go to plan. When I was working with some fellow production people I travelled to Australia where I was offered a share in a new company. The programme was to be inspirational about business and wellbeing. This I thought was just what I wanted to be involved in. I'm working in production, I'm making a series of inspirational programmes and travelling the world. We had an Oscar-nominated exec producer on board and this was it. Or so I thought. As I landed in Australia with a Producer we were met by one of the Australian team who drove us to his house. Now he was married to an ex-gangster from South Africa. While at their house she decided to tell me she had shot someone in South Africa and had to urinate on her hands to get rid of the gunshot residue. Ok……. Then they have a huge domestic argument, she tells me he's tried to kill her in the past and strangle her and I'm thinking is this shit for real. But hold on, it gets better. When we were sitting in the offices, walking towards us is this woman whom I'm told is the exec Producer. What, you mean that crackhead, waddling towards me with the googly eyes is the exec producer? Yep, that's her. She sits opposite me staring with these googly eyes, and a wonky mouth and I'm thinking "fuck she's going to leap over that desk and start eating my eyeballs" when she stands up and walks over to me and puts her hand on my shoulder and starts praying for me. I mean I know I'm no saint but I don't need Mrs land of the walking dead praying for me. The deal was to develop this project and I would be paid and have a share in the company. Safe to say no one had any intention of doing that. Thankfully after 4 weeks I made it back to good old Blighty and was no longer a part of the Australian Adams family. Result!

Thankfully though I learnt so much about production from my mate John who is a super talented film-maker and documentary filmmaker. We shot quite a few projects together, most of the time just the two of us whilst I also pursued my Photography. I always knew I would get into production and I'm sure people thought I was mad and it was all just a pipe dream. But here we are and now I'm in an award-winning television programme on Channel 4.

I talk about all my hippy guidance and my mates laugh at me but deep down I know they are looking at my cacao smoothie longing to secretly try it. But what I am referring to here is the list-making aspect that gives you a goal. Now if you want me to ditch the hippy vibes for a moment and touch on the scientific side briefly then no problem. Our brains have something called the reticular Activating System. The RAS is responsible for our wakefulness, our ability to focus, our fight-flight response, and how we ultimately perceive in our consciousness and is essentially a gatekeeper of information. It helps with organising information. It is a bundle of nerves at our brainstem that filters out unnecessary information so the important stuff gets through. It is the reason you learn a new word and then start hearing it everywhere. It's why you can tune out a crowd of people talking, yet immediately snap to attention when someone says your name. Your RAS takes what you focus on and creates a filter for it. It then sifts through the data and presents only the pieces of information that are important to you. The RAS helps you see what you want to see and in doing so, influences your actions. Fucking cool huh?

So by being clear on your intention you begin to notice what your RAS has been programmed to do. You find synchronicities. So if you care about positivity, for example, you will become more aware of and seek positivity. If you really want a pet goldfish and set your intent on getting one, you'll tune in to the right information that helps you do that.

So if you look at the law of attraction it doesn't seem so mystical after all if that isn't your thing. Focus on the bad things and you will invite negativity into your life. Focus on the good things and they will come to you because your brain is seeking them out.

Try this:

1. Think of a goal or situation you want to influence.
2. Now think about the experience or result you want to reach in regards to that goal/situation
3. Create a mental movie of how you picture that goal/situation ideally turning out in the future. Notice the sounds, conversations, visuals and details of that mental movie. Replay it often in your head.

The RAS is used in Neuro-Linguistic Programming (NLP) and getting that part of your brain on side. We can only process in our conscious mind around 5-7 things at a time and our brain has to filter out the billions of information that we do not need. The RAS will be looking to keep us safe. What we believe and notice is what we have programmed our RAS into.

If I say to you "look around the room and tell me everything that you see that is red, you would scan the room focusing on everything that is red. If I then say "Tell me everything that you just saw that was blue?" You will struggle as you have been focused on seeking everything that is red. Do you see where I am going with this? We attract and feel what we focus on. Good or bad. Wherever focus goes, energy flows.

If you wake up on a morning dreading your day your subconscious is kicking in and the likely outcome is you'll have a shit day. I make a point on a morning of visualising and changing my posture. I change my physiology. How many people are depressed and their shoulders are hunched forward, heads down with slow sad movements? Try changing your posture and you will feel a massive shift. The other thing is an absolute certainty that this is going to happen. No ifs no buts no maybe, you hit the day with absolute certainty and start to take action. If athletes or anyone else for that matter can get psyched up before an event why can't we do this with life? Why can't we visualise our day as being productive, and positive and change our energy? Rather than waking up and looking at the news or social media or some other shit on our phones, do some stretching, visualise your day and get ready to obliterate your list. Your to-do list is going to get smashed. You are pumped and ready to kick ass. Talk to yourself, hear yourself getting a pre-match talk. Imagine whatever you need to, play that music that excites you, listen to a podcast whilst brushing your hair, whatever works for you. Honestly, change your energy and you change your life. Change what you focus on and holy shit you are going to hit the next level of success. So whatever it is you have been putting off, have a brain dump, write that list and tick it off.

I got into a bad habit of procrastination or stopping a project before its completion and I couldn't understand why. Check this out. There is such a thing as fear of success. I know I know who would be fearful of success. Well, it's true. You can be afraid of what others will think of you if you become successful and start to earn big money for example. Would your family be jealous of you? Would your friends be envious and jealous? Could you trust anyone? Fear of success can be just as crippling as fear of failure. We can bring our ego into the mix and whilst our ego wants the adoration and praise, working on a project and striving for a goal our ego is on top, but when it's about to go go go our ego steps in and says "what if this fails?" Or "what if this is a huge success?" And we go all over the place and the project dies or is just shelved.

I was terrified of both. I have had some great successes and some almighty failures but now I have reached a point where I don't give two fucks about what others think. The handful of people that I give credence to don't matter. My family members that matter will be so supportive and the ones that have a problem don't matter. It's OK you're not even on my Christmas list mate. As for the fucktards that I give energy to and worry what they might think, well who cares. Crack on with your social media stalking and being miserable you're not on my Christmas list either. With this book, there are billions of people in this world that will benefit from me chirping on and hopefully will read this and make a massive shift in their lives. (Maybe not billions but a few would be great)

I always remember the phrase Paul Mort uses on his coaching programme"Do what you said you would" powerful stuff. I love it. We need to be accountable and if we say we are going to do something we need to follow it through. Find like-minded souls who are on the same mission and drive as you are. There are people out there either struggling or trying to get their shit together and you can bounce off each other. If you are having a wobble, the other could be firing on all cylinders and vice versa. Set yourself the goals and small wins if you are starting out rebuilding your life. These small wins will catapult you back into ass-kicking mode.

That is why I now love a list. Write that shit down.

LIFE AS A POLICE OFFICER

I did just short of 17 years as a Police Officer and what a journey that was. I was always going to pursue a career that was active and unpredictable. I did my school work experience with the army in York and loved playing sports, I was Captain of my house Football team and captain of the school rugby team winning the York and district final. I played for York All Blacks and there was nothing better than a freezing cold Sunday morning to play on a pitch that might as well have been concrete and watching as a team of neanderthal units rocked up with thighs bigger than my actual body. Now when you play rugby league in the north of England it produces some freaks of nature. How the actual fuck can a 17-year-old be twenty stone with a full beard, run 100m in two seconds and have shovel hands. Yeah well, you big freaks of nature let's see how you feel when you've got my Yorkshire hands hanging off your beard drowning you in a puddle from the melted concrete ice pitch. That's right Grizzly Adams you've met your match. When I played rugby or did anything I put my mind to I have this relentless mindset that no matter how hard it is no matter how many times I get knocked down I'm going to get back up and keep going. When I would do hill sprints I remember numerous times throwing up, but then I'd get my shit together and carry on. Apart from having my recent almighty, catastrophic, apocalyptic melting point, I guess this is where it stems from that even though I was struggling and felt like I had concrete blocks attached to my feet, there is this drive deep within me to get back up and keep going.

So while I was at college the Metropolitan Police were recruiting in London. My Dad drove me to London numerous times for all my assessments and interview and on the 14th of April 1996, I arrived at Hendon to be sworn in. Hendon was an incredible place apart from the recruit blocks we stayed in. The place should have been condemned as being unfit to house anyone. My room had a bed and a desk and a sink and communal toilets and showers that had definitely gone past their best before date. My room had A1 sheets of paper on the walls with law and Police powers in multi-coloured writing to study for my exams. I did get a couple of awards at Training college, one voted for by my classmates for being a good egg and another one that I can't remember what for. I found the medal recently while sorting through all my old stuff with my commendations. I did have aspirations to climb the ladder and was very much into studying. I had all my study books and law books and would be a mentor to new probationers joining our team despite only completing my probation. I loved my job. I would take every call, nick anyone and everyone, and I was always the first to work. I would get in early and use the gym and then I would research crimes and intelligence and make a list of recently stolen cars and memorise their registrations. I was always the last to leave after wracking up a ridiculous amount of crime reports but I loved it. I played Rugby for the Police and whenever there was a family get-together or new people are introduced my younger brother always gives the example of when we played North Yorkshire Police and I broke someone's nose. Now his version is slightly different to mine in that I broke an old man's nose. My version is this gentleman buried his face into me and got a nose bleed.

I did have a reputation in the Police and somehow got the nickname

Bashmore which then became Bash. When you've accumulated a few complaints from scumbags having a nickname called 'BASH' doesn't do you any favours. When you are faced with a daily onslaught of shitbags wanting to punch your lights out, it does just become your 'norm' but having said that I do like a good punch up. Not though when you punch someone square on the forehead. The result is a broken hand that looks like a claw. I did momentarily have a comedy hand but holy shit when they put it back together it hurt. I'm sure I had a Victorian-era Doctor. Here you go Mr Cashmore chew on this bit of plastic and we will tug and pull your hand back together again. FUUUUUUUCK ME SIDEWAYS................. All I could think is "You're the devil incarnate" You would think the lesson I learnt is not to fight. Oh no, the lesson I learnt is not to punch people in the face. I mean seriously, what the fuck is wrong with me? So I perfected the body shot at the boxing gym. As I'm right-handed I trained relentlessly to throw a body shot with my left. Not that I took this shit seriously of course. I mean watching relentless Ricky Hatton fights, who in my opinion is the king of the body shot kind of took up a lot of my free time. To be fair in my younger years I think I thought I was invincible.

You do deal with some crazy shit as a Police Officer and it can give you a twisted outlook on life. But realistically not everyone is a bad person and you shouldn't let a career or situation give you a distorted outlook on life. Fuck ups are life's training ground. Everyone fucks up at some point but it's not the event but our response to it.

We all have free will and we make decisions at the time which we think are right, but there is absolutely no point at all for the sake of your sanity or your health to dwell on them. So you might be at a crossroads in your life and thinking where do I go from here? Well my friend there is an abundance of explorations and roads to travel out there. Don't let life and what has gone before you hold any bearing on you. The only day that matters is now. RIGHT

FUCKING NOW! When I joined the 'Old Bill' I thought I was going to make a difference. I thought every day was going to be adrenaline and excitement, I thought I was going to save people, I thought I was going to protect people, which I did, but I also had a burning desire to start my own business and be creative. I would never have guessed in a million years that my job as a Police Officer would facilitate my dream job of working in television. The universe can be one strange place and takes you on many twists and turns. I did see a lot of unhappy souls as a Police Officer and it's easy to see why. With the relentless financial cuts, extra workload, and zero life outside of the job, so many officers would be counting down the hours until their shift finishes and worst of all counting down the years, months and days until they retired. That is some scary shit right there. Wishing your life away until the day you retire. You are so unhappy that you are ticking off the days until you leave your employment and retire. I know so many people who have reached retirement and are still not happy but even worse have sadly passed away and never even got the chance to enjoy their retirement. There is a phrase that if you can't change the circumstance change your attitude towards it. Whilst that is true you can still make changes. Train your mindset to be grateful and if it's a career change you're looking for there has never been a greater time to start your own business. I have read countless examples of people in careers in their 30's, 40's and even later in life that have just said 'fuck this I'm making a change and started their business. Age doesn't matter at all. Youtube influencers are making good money, there are tech millionaires in their twenties, James Dyson didn't hit the jackpot until later in life building bagless vacuum cleaners, solicitors retraining to be plumbers and city workers becoming photographers.

Funny that when you're on the bones of your arse the people that lift you are very few and far between but when you are super successful and flying high every man and his dog want to be your friend.

There is another side to all of this and it is helping others in need. We all get so busy with our hectic lives that we can sometimes forget to send a message or arrange to meet our friends and family even for a coffee. Don't get too caught up in life that it passes you by. Winston Churchill famously said, "We make a living by what we get, we make a life by what we give".

But back to being careful whom you ask for advice. Did you ever see the UK version of Dragons Den where a guy entered the 'Den' and pitched his business called the TANGLE TEEZER. It is a hairbrush that detangles your hair. Well, he was basically ridiculed by the entire panel of Dragons, but he went away and his hairbrush is sold all over the world and he is now extremely wealthy. If someone is overweight and unfit are you going to take their advice on how to get a six-pack? More and more people are venturing into the world of business and startups like never before. Don't be fooled by thinking you need a university degree to be successful in business either. So many successful entrepreneurs have overcome extreme adversity and difficulties in life. Richard Branson left school at sixteen and is a Billionaire, Sir Alan Sugar wasn't born with a silver spoon in his mouth and the author of Harry Potter was a single mother recently divorced and would sit in a coffee shop writing her book.

It might be that you want a career change that involves learning a new skill or retraining. I know of solicitors who have retrained as plumbers and earn more money, I know of Police Officers who have studied and left the force to become solicitors. There are courses available online that you can qualify for and you can also get help with funding or student loans that get repaid through your tax bill. So my point is don't feel like you are trapped in a job for the rest of your life and feel like there is no way out. Because trust me there is. You just need that inspiration and courage to do it. The reason the term 'side hustle' is becoming so popular is that it is the ones who have commitments like children and mortgages and taking the leap from something that is financially secure to sailing in unknown water and not knowing if that contract is going to come to fruition is daunting and I completely understand. We have all made mistakes but we cannot let our mistakes define us or let fear rule us.

Fear is one thing that separates most of us. Nearly every aspect of our lives from relationships to careers to upsetting our parents by making certain decisions. Let's look at relationships. How many people do you know that attract the opposite sex without any problem at all? I bet you even know people who might have been blessed with a face for radio (no offence intended radio peeps out there) who just seem to always have a rather attractive person on their arm. Normally they are funny fuckers and seem to make them laugh until 'BOOM' They're naked. Most of these people are also relentless in asking the opposite sex out until they get a 'yes'. They have zero fear of rejection. They just move on. I do wonder how many people out there have missed that golden opportunity of finding Mr or Mrs Right simply by being fearful of rejection. Seriously what the actual fuck have you got to lose? Nothing. Absolutely fuck all. I know as a species we have all of these survival instincts but you need to tell that inner fear in you to FUCK OFF!

IMPOSTOR SYNDROME

Ok here comes a deep bit for you to ponder. There is something called imposter syndrome. Even though you are extremely successful you just feel like a fraud and it's like you can't internalise your experiences of success. Imposter syndrome was first identified in 1978 by psychologists Pauline Rose Clance and Suzanne Imes. Psychologist Audrey Ervin states that imposter syndrome can affect anyone who isn't able to internalise and own their successes.

"Perfectionists" set extremely high expectations for themselves, and even if they meet 99% of their goals, they're going to feel like failures. Any small mistake will make them question their competence.

"Experts" feel the need to know every piece of information before they start a project and constantly look for new certifications or training to improve their skills. They won't apply for a job if they don't meet all the criteria in the posting, and they might be hesitant to ask a question in class or speak up in a meeting at work because they're afraid of looking stupid if they don't already know the answer.

When the natural genius has to struggle or work hard to accomplish something, he or she thinks this means they aren't good enough.

They are used to skills coming easily, and when they have to put in the effort, their brain tells them that's proof they're an impostor.

"Soloists" feel they have to accomplish tasks on their own, and if they need to ask for help, they think that means they are a failure or a fraud.

I think what we need to do is stop fucking comparing ourselves to others. I would constantly compare myself to others and constantly question if I am good enough or how can I be the best. I am the King of research but I'm not sure this is the best trait to have. It's almost a compulsive disorder I have. I will sit and study and learn and read and watch videos until I know this stuff inside and out. Yet I still wonder if I have all of the knowledge I need. What a head fuck.

I have read that people who experience imposter syndrome also tend not to talk about how they are feeling with anyone and suffer in silence, just as do those with social anxiety disorder. To get past this you should ask yourself some questions such as "What core beliefs do I hold about myself?" and "Must I be perfect for others to approve of me?"
They say perfectionism plays a significant role in imposter syndrome and you may procrastinate due to your high standards. How often have you put something off like a call until the "right time?"

So as I'm not a psychiatrist or trained professional all I'm going to say is take it by the balls and squeeze those fuckers. Squeeze away, and stop comparing yourself to others and worrying about what they think or will say. Who gives two fucks what a colleague or anyone of insignificance thinks. Who cares if there is a whats app chat group where they have a non-stop moan fest and slag people off? While they are bitching and whining you will be doing something incredible. I pretty much know there will be some bitching and whining that I have written this and most probably a whats app chat group but you know what, that same chat group have probably bought this book, read it, got to this section and thought "fuck, I've been busted" but you know what, I love it. They have spent money on it, devoted time to it and discussed it. Fucking bingo as far as I'm concerned.

Who cares what the negative freaks out there think? James Blunt is brilliant on social media in dealing with the negativity and I saw one come back on Twitter where he replied "Mortgage-free". Hahahahaha how good is that? There are going to be keyboard warriors out there slagging people off but jealousy is a bad trait to have. Who has seen the film "The Pursuit of Happiness?" Everyone knows the section of the film where the main character tells his son to never let anyone tell him that it can't be done. It's ok to speak to people and let them be your sounding board, but be careful whom you choose. You will learn over time who doesn't want you to succeed and who is blowing smoke up your arse. My advice is to smile, nod, agree and do whatever the fuck you were going to do anyway.

FINDING YOUR PASSION

Who wants to live a life of quiet desperation and go to the grave with a song still in them?

We hear entrepreneurs talk a lot about finding your passion. But if you find something you are passionate about you will never work a day in your life. You will be working on it, breathing every minute of the day and thinking about it. What is it though that stops us? Is it fear? Fear of failure, fear of what others will think, fear of success? There is always a common thread when faced with death and that is what do I regret not doing with my life or what would I have done differently?

Is Insanity *doing the same thing over and over again and expecting different results?*

We need to look at whether we are flogging a dead horse or adopting Einstein's Insanity theory. If it's a dead horse then clearly it's getting binned off, but if we are venturing into Einstein's Insanity theory we need to look more closely. I think Einstein's theory applies to so many things from relationships to work to even training in the gym. But doing the same thing over and over is just perfectionism right?

Let's go off tangent a little and look at our health and going to the gym. We all (well most of us) want that six-pack and to look good. We are flooded with magazine articles and films where models, singers, and actors look in great shape, but more often than not it is a gruelling training and diet regime to get in shape for the project. How many actors have undertaken training to prepare for a film role and then as soon as the film is finished it is time to grab that doughnut and not worry about getting up at 5 am to eat boiled chicken and complete an intense workout? The driving force was a 'GOAL' to get in shape for their job. We all do it to some degree, whether it is to lose some insulation around the belly when we go on holiday, to lose the Christmas pudding that is hanging over our jeans or getting ready to put on your wedding dress or wedding suit so your new husband or wife thinks "yes, you're getting it tonight".

So what am I getting at here? Well, we all need a goal or a vision, something to aim and strive for. Don't be a ship at sea with no direction. Don't simply float along. We all need direction. Find it and make a plan.

Now that then brings me to consistency. This my friends is the key to all success in my opinion. BE CONSISTENT. Let's go back to the gym scenario for a minute. Now if we are inconsistent and eat healthy then eat shit, do a workout one day, then have a week off, get hammered four days a week, then work out two days the following week you're probably not going to achieve the results you want. So don't float along, set out your goals, set out your battle plan and go and fuck shit up.............

Finding your passion can mean so many things, so hear me out. You might just be the most incredible salesperson and this might be what you are passionate about but it is also what drives you. From sourcing your prospective clients, and forging relationships to securing the sale. You might find a product out there that you believe so passionately in that you just have to be a part of it and by selling it you see the rewards of money in your account but also the satisfaction of closing the sale.

It might be that you are in a shit job at the moment and thinking "What the fuck" but you have a passion that you spend most of your spare time pursuing, learning, perfecting the craft but the key is how to monetise it. This is now known as 'THE SIDE HUSTLE'.

Finding your passion might not just be your job. Your job might actually be Ok and we all need to earn a living. Finding your passion might be something on the side, but what normally happens is someone finds and discovers their passion and money follows. It doesn't start with 'money' that just seems to be a byproduct. I have had countless conversations with people who have hit what outsiders call 'The Jackpot' and the majority say that the money came afterwards. How many people started making cupcakes, started knitting, or making t-shirts, or painting and then it just steamrolls into something incredible that impacts others? A hobby that turns into a business that impacts others is going to make you feel amazing. All of a sudden we have gone from purely existing by going to work, coming home, and watching TV whilst drinking a glass of wine to unwind to feel inspired and excited about learning a new skill, a new language, or starting a new course. The common phrase is "I don't have time" and whilst time is precious, if you are passionate about something and want to make a change you will make time. How many hours do we spend in the car driving and we could be learning g a new language, listening to an inspiring audiobook (like this one) or listening to something that will expand your current knowledge base? When the passion and excitement comes, butterflies will be in your stomach, your physiology will change and you will begin to smile more. It will be like walking around with a coat hanger in your mouth your smile will be that big.

THE SIDE HUSTLE

The Side Hustle is seen as something everyone wants to do now and if you don't have one you might even be telling people you have. Because having a side hustle is what the king of side hustles himself preaches. We all know that guy from social media who shows you how to flip items and buy them cheap and sell them, he shows you how to target potential clients using social media and location hashtags and I think the main thing he promotes is you've just got to do it and not be afraid. Who cares about that minority of negativity or jealousy? Fuck them.

Let me use myself as an example. I love cameras. I mean I literally love them. I love being able to shoot videos and take photographs. I think about it day and night. I see images and art that inspire me and I'm constantly trying to better myself and improve. Years ago I thought I was pretty good but when I look back I am a completely different photographer and videographer now. I would over-post-produce my still images when actually less is more. I didn't shoot in full manual mode back then which I do now but it has taken me years of practice to instantly know the conditions I'm shooting, to know the settings I need from my camera and what lens I need to get the image that I envisage in my mind.

I have lost count of the number of books I have read, videos I have watched, magazines I have saved in my office to the thousands of photos I have taken to improve. I constantly take photos of my children. If there is ever a training ground to nail the shot and get the focus it is children's portrait photography. I have taken countless children's portraits ranging from triplets, and twins to the hyperactive child who will never in a million years sit still. I have had a family come to me and at the end of the session leave thinking they have no useable photo's when in fact they have loads. There is no way on earth I'm not getting the shot for them.

So this is something I love and I am passionate about, it's capturing a memory, a moment in time. I think it's the emotion that the photograph brings back that is such a powerful thing.

Yet there is something else. It is the phrase of finding your Dharma. Which is essentially finding your purpose in life. Your Dharma is your true calling and what you were put here to do. Ancient yoga texts describe dharma as inner wisdom, or cosmic guidance that governs not only you and me as individuals but the entire universe as well.

So in a spiritual context, we all have a soul purpose. More than one job or career. They say that often our dharma comes through obstacles as well as joy. When these deep shadows show up and send us to the pit mostly we can find clarity and purpose. There is a circle that is split into categories of Teacher, Artist, Warrior, Entrepreneur, Researcher, Activist, Visionary, Nurturer, Entertainer and when we look at these we can find ourselves in some of them. We might have elements of these and find out what our dharma is. Mostly I think we all know deep down.

Firstly pay attention to synchronicity. I know we touched on the RAS earlier and that is science-based but I want you to pay attention to your spiritual side. Most people miss the opportunity and miss the signs and clues and if you pay attention to what is showing up in your life. Follow callings or instincts. There are those tiny feelings when you want to do something even if it doesn't make sense. The feeling isn't coming from your mind it is your instinct or intuition. Your logical brain is just trying to process this. If there is a calling it is often preparation for your dharma. Your instincts can never fail you. You also need to know when to let go. Sometimes your mind can be pushing for you to continue but is your intuition telling you to let go? The path of dharma is not straight, that's why you will hear life is full of ups and downs. If you try and master your own dharma you will drive yourself crazy, for you to be able to understand it you need to listen to your heart. Your heart and logical brain will constantly be in conflict. Practice meditation and connect with a greater source and quiet the mind and be ready. Whom do you admire? Whom do you find inspiring? What is it you admire about these people?

I have only just started to explore yoga and whilst I am no expert I want to understand dharma. It's about having a life purpose, learning the life lessons, seeing those repeating patterns and not being sucked into groundhog day. Most people don't know what their dharma is and are trying to figure it out. Part of figuring out what our dharma is; is getting out into the world and finding out what makes us feel good and what doesn't and what sits with us.
I have sat on the mission to write a book to help and inspire others for so long. It took me to hit a personal nightmare to finish it. I also finished my PT course and consumed so much self-development information I want to share it with everyone.

I thought that my life purpose was being creative. Whilst I love the creative process I feel compelled to help others. I have made some shit mistakes in life and hopefully, I can rebalance these mistakes by giving something back.

Similar to dharma there is a Japanese philosophy called Ickigai which stands for 'reason for being', Ikigai can help us determine what it is.

Many people fall into a depression based purely on their jobs. If it is possible to change our job and find something with passion and purpose then this is life-changing. We must pick something we are good at and it must be something we love to do and the world should need it and lastly, we need to get paid and see some financial reward.

Everyone has a different skill set. There is nature and nurture where we can learn new skills but we also have an inborn characteristic that makes different people more suitable for different things. We may be different in motor skills, empathy, physical strength etc. What are we naturally good at? We need to experience a flow state. Listen to your gut and intuition. What we love to do isn't necessarily Ikigai it is our passion. Is it what the world needs? Jobs that are looked down on by some are highly important.

All of this is different to doing something because of ego. It is finding something that is fulfilling. When I say I am passionate about making memories and being creative and whilst I love taking photos of my children and making family memories is this going to be my full-time career? Is this going to be my dharma? Well, I'm constantly being pulled into wellness and health. I mean constantly. Mostly starting with my own journey and understanding more and consuming information. Can I combine the two? It just might be that I can utilise both and marry these into finding my unique dharma.

My first real venture into wellness initially started when I would break out in excema or my stomach would look like I was 9 months pregnant. I would hit up the GP and basically get a blank look. I started researching the effects of dairy and quickly came to the conclusion this was a trigger. I also looked at wheat and gluten long before it became trendy to be gluten-free, and yes this had a massive improvement on my joints and pregnant belly. I became obsessed with health and wellness but somehow became lost and slipped back into my old ways. I would read Buddhist teachings, NLP, and mindset books, and listen to inspiring lectures but then it just stopped and I can't even tell you how. I became lost. I had clearly found my Ikigai or dharma and binned it off. I ended up going back to this character who wasn't me and as a consequence almost cost me my sanity. I was suppressing who I am.

I would lay next to my partner and she would place her hands on me and imagine so much love and light entering my body that I would feel these enormous waves of emotion rush over me. I knew what she was doing and could feel it yet I would suppress this emotion stored in me. It was like an energy healing, the most surreal experience.

I touched on signs and synchronicities earlier and one of the most bizarre ones is a Facebook message I received from someone I don't know. It was a Facebook messenger request who initially contacted me with something and I blocked him. I thought I don't know you and don't want spam. But bizarrely even though I blocked him I received another message from him. The message was a screenshot of a conversation and it read ' You bet we are a website filled with helpful resources and our mission is to help enable writers to grow their skills so they can publish their books and get them into the hands of readers. There was no click through no nothing to spam me or get my details. I'm confused because I thought I had blocked this person. Indeed the website looks legitimate and so I carried on and got to work being disciplined in getting this book finished.

I have been flying through this book and set myself a deadline and was aiming for 25'000 words. The reason for this is I came across, by accident again a writer who explained how many words a book like this can have, and it is around 25'000. Signs and synchronicities are everywhere. I needed to lift some major blockages though in order to let the words come out. I needed to not care what insignificant others thought and I needed to reprogram my mind from sadness and regret and guilt and forgive others and forgive myself or at least ask for forgiveness and just be at peace within myself.

Within this journey of coming back from Shitsville, I genuinely believe I have found my dharma. My quest to help others. It has a double side to it. I get to progress and develop myself whilst helping others. I get to use my life experience to fully empathise with others. I get the chance to give back. What an absolute winner.

If you are stuck in a never-ending loop of Monday morning stress and are desperate to make a change to any aspect of your life, I want you to know it is possible. Anything is possible. If you want to take the island you have to burn your boat. You know what I mean, everything is on the other side of fear. Fear of the unknown, fear of success, fear of failure, but you know what, fuck fear. Make the decision to start today. Just brain dump, write that list, find something to be grateful for and go after whatever it is with passion, drive, excitement and relentless pursuit. If you decide to get in shape, don't tell anyone, just do it. If you decide to study and retrain, just do it. You've got this.

FAMILY

Family to me is the most important thing in the world, yet something I have probably royally made an absolute fuck up with. Out of everything though I am blessed with three incredible children. My children inspire me every single day and I cannot even express in words how much love I have for them. Just the thought of my children makes me smile.

I was lucky enough to meet someone with whom I thought we would be together forever. This person was incredibly supportive and she would lay her hands on my head and try to take away all my fear and anxiety from me, but when you are suffering from constant anxiety and your mind is telling you to stop projecting this onto them and you are on autopilot to self destruct you do the unthinkable and pull the pin out on a massive grenade in your mind.

I am normally a driven, enthusiastic supportive man but just like a computer that is overheating and malfunctioning, I malfunctioned on an epic level. If only there was a way to unplug, pause for 20 seconds and then turn it back on I would have been very very grateful.

So here I am, king fuck up who is getting his shit together but if I hadn't gone through such pain and suffering in my mind I wouldn't be writing this book, I wouldn't be on a mission to help and inspire others to get up from the canvas and attack life with every fibre of their being.

If you are suffering right now, trust me it doesn't last. If there are situations or people that have hurt you or you have hurt them, don't carry that shit around with you. You need to know that you are not alone and to reach out. Reaching out is the biggest step you will ever take. Tyson Fury the heavyweight champion of the world freely admits he still struggles. This is a giant of a man who was a heavyweight champ and then put on so much weight and was on a path to self-destruct. He explains he was crying so much his shirt was soaked through and praying to God to help him. He then starts the journey to getting his belts and becoming the undisputed heavyweight champ again. Ricky Hatton another world champion boxer freely admits his struggles, Mike Tyson again another Heavyweight champion struggled and in interviews talks about how he overcame his demons. These are not just anyone these are fighters who have had fame, money and success and still struggle. So each of us on this planet is unique and should never be in a situation where we feel we can't speak out. Fuck that, yes you can.

There is the phrase having a brain dump' I have embraced that. Having a brain dump is the first step. Because you know what, it might not be just one 'big' thing' you are trying to process it might be one of 20 things you are trying to process.

All of the topics I cover in this book we can adopt and always remember it's not the situation it's our response to it. Your happiness starts with you. When you master these two things you can conquer the world.

But back to family. When the world is all fucked and friends come and go, who are the ones we need to let know that we are there and we love them? Our family but we also have those friends that come under the family umbrella and may as well be blood. That little text just to check in and see if they are OK, that little card to say thank you, that invite for lunch in your garden or picnic in the park. These sentiments cost nothing if very little yet mean so much and change someone's day.

I do believe we should never go to sleep on an argument and checking in with your parents and making memories is so important. I think we take the fact we think our parents will be around forever. If the pandemic taught us anything it was that a simple hug to our grandparents and parents and loved ones that were the most valuable thing we can give and one of the things we missed the most. I am still blessed with my amazing family and I also have friends that have listened to me ramble on including my best mate that might as well be my blood Brother and a family that is just wonderful. If shit hits the fan and you are praying for a miracle, sometimes we can be blessed with real-life Angels.

I also want to sign off this book with the same thing I started with. If you are lucky enough to find a weirdo, never let them go. I can say that I royally cocked that one up, but I fully appreciate that some people come into our lives for a reason a season or a lifetime, some as real-life Angels, and some will stay with us forever. Tell the ones you love that you love them, smile more, give that hug, say sorry and also accept an apology, make peace and live a happy and content life.

If something ignites your soul, listen to your heart. Your heart and your gut will lead you in the right direction and your brain will try and process those feelings. Love will conquer all. Energy is real so remember you are a magnet and if you are emitting love and kindness you will get it back.

Go out into the world, believe you are a magnet and live the life you want and trust that everything will come to you at the right time. Be in a flow state my friend and miracles will happen.

You've got this.

It's GAME ON MUTHERFUCKERS.

ABOUT THE AUTHOR

Paul is a former highly commended Police Officer and member of the most effective Robbery Squad in London. Having received commendations for dedication and professionalism to disarming a gunman where shots were fired he then went on to establish a successful boxing initiative working with underprivileged young people to prevent gang violence and knife crime. Paul was also a bodyguard protecting UHNW and celebrity clients where he protected and saved the life of a celebrity. Paul was then cast in the Channel 4 series HUNTED as a Hunter and has since trained as a camera operator and is a licensed drone pilot.

Paul is a qualified boxing coach and level 3 PT and has studied how nutrition and exercise are vitally important for mental wellbeing. Paul incorporates mindset and has studied NLP, CBT, and Meditation and now works with corporations and companies to reduce workplace stress and illness and provides workshops and presentations.

To contact Paul for workshops and presentations visit
www.paulcashmore.com

Printed in Great Britain
by Amazon

14815332R00058